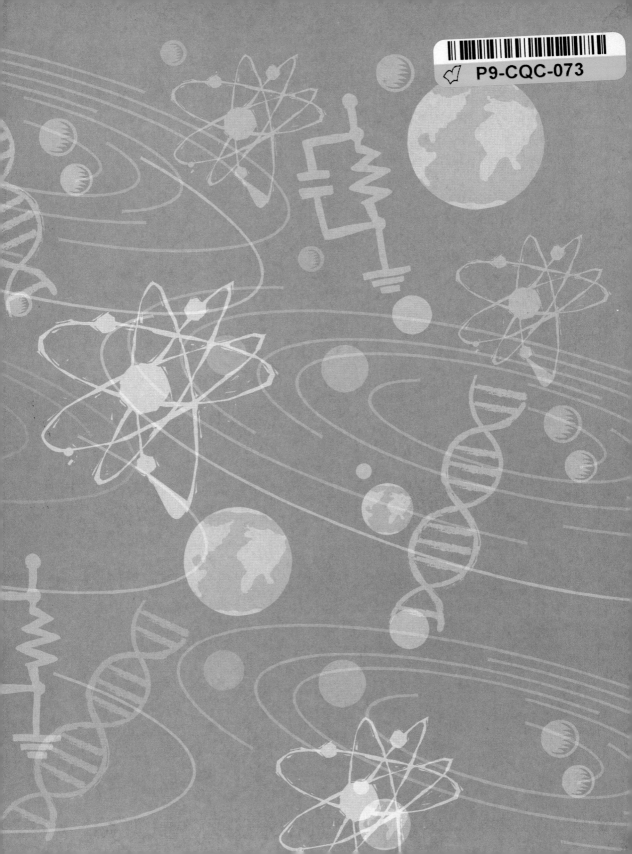

Cells

by Kimberly Fekany Lee

Science Contributor
Sally Ride Science
Science Consultants
Thomas R. Ciccone, Science Educator
Ronald Edwards, Ph.D., Science Educator

First hardcover edition published in 2009 by
Compass Point Books
151 Good Counsel Drive
P.O. Box 669
Mankato, MN 56002-0669

Editor: Jennifer VanVoorst
Designer: Heidi Thompson
Editorial Contributor: Sue Vander Hook

Art Director: LuAnn Ascheman-Adams
Creative Director: Keith Griffin
Editorial Director: Nick Healy
Managing Editor: Catherine Neitge

 This book was manufactured with paper containing at least 10 percent post-consumer waste.

Library of Congress Cataloging-in-Publication Data
Lee, Kimberly Fekany.
 Cells / by Kimberly Fekany Lee.
    p. cm. — (Mission: Science)
 Includes index.
 ISBN 978-0-7565-3954-2 (library binding)
1. Cells—Juvenile literature. I. Title. II. Series.
 QH582.5.L42 2009
 571.6—dc22   2008007719

Visit Compass Point Books on the Internet at *www.compasspointbooks.com*
or e-mail your request to *custserv@compasspointbooks.com*

Table of Contents

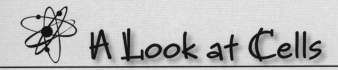

A Look at Cells

Have you ever seen a cell? A cell is the smallest unit of life—the basic structure for every living thing. Cells are called the building blocks of life.

Some living things, such as tiny bacteria, are made up of only one cell. But plants and animals have trillions of cells that perform specialized jobs. The larger the organism, the more cells it has. The blue whale, the largest animal on Earth, has 1,000 times more cells than a human being.

Most cells are so small that they can be seen only under a microscope. English scientist Robert Hooke (1635–1703) was the first person to see a cell. In 1665, while observing a thin slice of cork under a microscope, he saw tiny boxlike shapes surrounded by walls. The walls and boxes reminded him of the tiny rooms, or cells, that monks lived in,

so he named them *cellulae*. The word is Latin for "little rooms." Nine years later, Dutch scientist Anton van Leeuwenhoek (1632–1723) observed a living cell for the first time under a microscope.

The work of these and other scientists over the centuries led to the development of the Cell Theory in the 1830s. German scientists Matthias Schleiden, Theodor Schwann, and Rudolf Virchow are credited with independently developing the Cell Theory. The theory states three things: all living things are made up of one or more cells; cells are the basic unit of life; and all cells come from other cells.

Did You Know?

The average human is made of 60 trillion to 100 trillion cells.

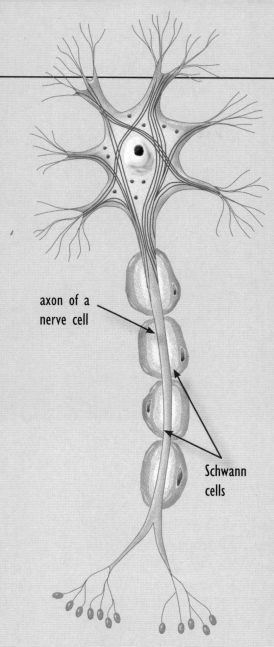

axon of a
nerve cell

Schwann
cells

Schwann cells spiral around
the axon as many as 100
times to provide protection.

Theodor Schwann
(1810—1882)

Living organisms have many
kinds of cells. Some form organs,
such as the stomach or lungs.
Others watch for bacteria and
viruses. Muscle cells allow
humans and animals to move.
Nerve cells transmit signals,
telling the brain what the eyes are
seeing or what the skin is feeling.

When scientist Theodor Schwann
was studying long, spindly
nerve cells under a microscope,
he observed some special cells.
They spiraled around the axon,
the nerve cell's long taillike
projection. The many layers of
these cells provide protection
and insulation for the axon. He
called them Schwann cells.

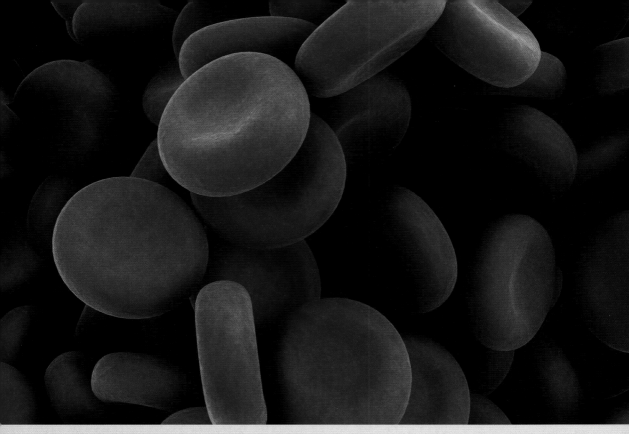

▲ Red blood cells transport oxygen from the lungs to the tissues and return carbon dioxide to the lungs.

Cell Shape and Size

Plants and animals both have many types of cells, each with a unique shape that matches its special job. In animals, red blood cells look like small bowl-shaped discs. They are soft and flexible, allowing them to squeeze through the smallest blood vessels called capillaries. Their shape allows them to travel quickly, delivering necessary oxygen to the body.

Animals also have muscle cells, which are long and thin. Nerve cells send signals to and from the brain. They look like an octopus with spindly arms stretching out from the body in the center. Some nerve cells that control the farthest extremities of the body are very long.

Cells also come in many sizes. Large cells have

functions that are different from those of small cells. You may think that large cells are better than small cells, but the opposite is true. Sometimes small cells are more efficient because they can squeeze through tiny areas. If cells get too big, they are not as effective. A larger surface area means that there is more area for substances to enter and exit cells. A smaller inside area means that substances have a smaller distance to travel to get from one side of a cell to the other.

How Big Is That?

Most human cells are about 20 micrometers across. These cells are so small that it would take 10,000 human cells to cover the head of a pin.

Long Cells

Some nerve cells in your body are more than 3 feet (1 meter) long. The sciatic nerve starts at the base of your spine and extends all the way to the tips of your toes.

◀ A nerve cell can have many appendages.

Plant Cells and Animal Cells

Plant cells and animal cells are surrounded by a cell membrane. It acts as a gatekeeper, controlling what goes in and out of a cell. Some substances move easily through the cell membrane, while others are not allowed in or out.

The cell membrane of a plant cell is surrounded by a cell wall. Cell walls are stronger than cell membranes, but they are not as flexible. When you water a plant, the water moves into the cells. As the cell fills up with water, the cell membrane pushes against the rigid cell wall. This gives support to the plant. Animal cells do not have cell walls. If an animal cell receives too much water, the cell will burst.

Another difference between plant and animal cells is how they get their energy. Plant cells make their own food using the energy from sunlight. Animals get fuel for their cells from the foods they eat.

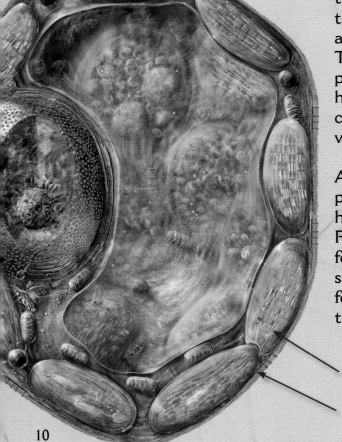

cell membrane

cell wall

Robert Brown
(1773—1858)

Robert Brown was a botanist who studied thousands of plants in the early 1800s. He was born in Scotland but spent three and a half years in Australia collecting about 3,400 plant species. About 2,000 of them were new plant species that Brown identified and named. Some were named after him.

Brown made many notable discoveries in the field of cell biology. He found that all plant cells have a round structure in the middle. He named the structure the nucleus. Scientists later discovered that the nucleus controls a cell's activities. It also holds DNA, the cell's genetic material.

Did You Know?

Humans cannot easily digest plant cell walls. When we eat plants, the cell walls pass through the digestive system as fiber. We don't digest fiber, but it scrubs away other matter that can't be digested.

Moving In and Out of Cells

Substances must travel in and out of cells. Tiny openings in the cell membrane let these substances in or out. Diffusion is one way cells take in nutrients and rid themselves of waste. In diffusion, substances move from an area of high concentration to an area of low concentration.

It's like dropping food coloring into a cup of water. When you first drop it in, the food coloring stays in a ball. But in time, the food coloring spreads throughout the water, and all the water gets colored. The color has moved from an area of high concentration (the drop of food coloring) to an area of low concentration (the surrounding water).

Cell diffusion is usually a slow process. Sometimes it is made easier by proteins, which make a channel through the cell membrane. This kind of diffusion is called facilitated diffusion.

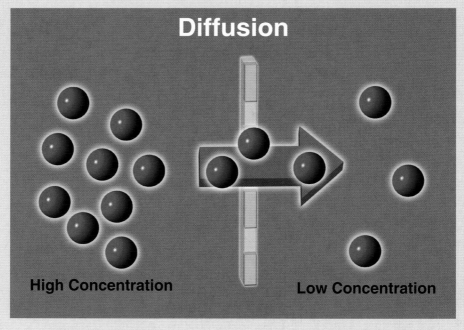

Diffusion

High Concentration

Low Concentration

Diffusion lets molecules move from one side of a cell membrane to the other until an equal number of molecules are on both sides of the membrane.

Can You Smell It?

Diffusion is not just for cells. When you smell an odor from across the room, it means that substances have traveled through the air by diffusion.

Food coloring dropped into water is an example of diffusion.

Cells take in nutrients and expel waste through diffusion.

Cytoplasm and Organelles

Plant and animal cells are filled with cytoplasm, a fluid like gelatin. It is made of cytosol, which is like a special soup that has everything the cell needs to live.

Inside the cytoplasm are many different cell parts,

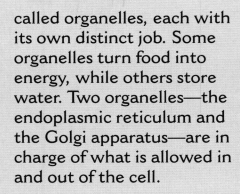

called organelles, each with its own distinct job. Some organelles turn food into energy, while others store water. Two organelles—the endoplasmic reticulum and the Golgi apparatus—are in charge of what is allowed in and out of the cell.

Most organelles are separated from the cytosol by a membrane, a skinlike substance that only lets in what the organelle needs. Everything else is kept outside.

One kind of organelle in a plant cell is the chloroplast. Chloroplasts turn sunlight into energy that the rest of the cell can use. Animal cells do not have chloroplasts. Animals get their energy from eating other things.

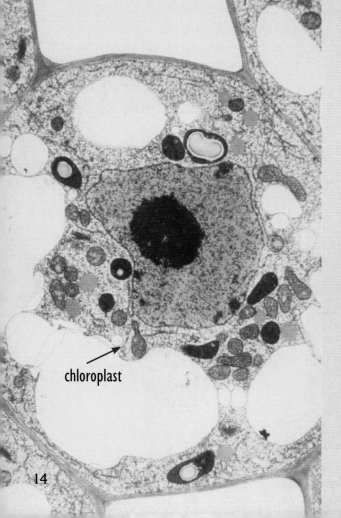

chloroplast

◀ plant cell

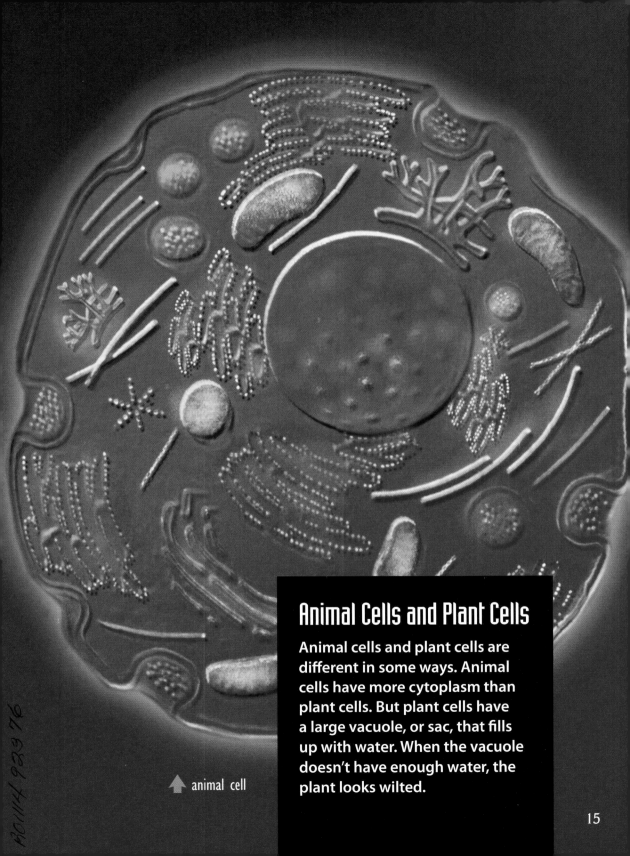

animal cell

Animal Cells and Plant Cells

Animal cells and plant cells are different in some ways. Animal cells have more cytoplasm than plant cells. But plant cells have a large vacuole, or sac, that fills up with water. When the vacuole doesn't have enough water, the plant looks wilted.

15

The Control Center

The nucleus of a cell is often called the control center. Every part of a cell gets directions from the nucleus. How does the nucleus supervise these activities? Inside the nucleus are genes located on long threadlike structures called chromosomes. Genes are made of a molecule called deoxyribonucleic acid (DNA) that contains a code for all the functions of a cell. Genes "tell" cells what to do. Chromosomes, genes, and DNA are what make each species and each individual unique.

The nucleus is surrounded by a nuclear membrane. Tiny openings in the membrane called pores allow some substances to pass in and out, but DNA never leaves the nucleus. Information carried by DNA is transferred to another molecule called ribonucleic acid (RNA) that can leave the nucleus.

ribosomes

nucleus

pore

chromosome

RNA

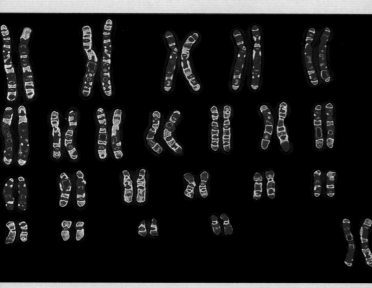

Humans have 23 pairs of chromosomes.

RNA then gives instructions to ribosomes, which help assemble proteins. A cell's proteins affect what it is like and what it can do. It all starts with DNA.

DNA curls into a shape called a double helix.

Unique DNA

Each species has a different number of chromosomes that are organized in pairs. The cells of a fruit fly have eight chromosomes, or four pairs. Dog cells have 78 chromosomes, or 39 pairs. Each human being has 46 chromosomes, or 23 pairs, with a set of genes unique to that individual. Because people have unique genes, DNA can be used to help solve crimes. Police can figure out a person's DNA by studying his or her blood, fingernails, hair, or other parts. They can then match the DNA to evidence found at the scene of a crime.

Energy in Cells

Have you ever wondered how we get the energy to walk, run, eat, and even sleep? Energy comes from our cells. It is the job of organelles called mitochondria to change the food we eat into energy that cells can use. This is called cellular respiration.

After the mitochondria release energy, the cells use the energy to build new proteins, move molecules around the cell, and make more cells. Plants also have mitochondria, but they get their energy from the sun.

Plant cells also use chloroplasts to produce energy. Chloroplasts contain a pigment called chlorophyll that makes the plant green. But it also absorbs energy from the sun or other sources of light. The chloroplast uses that energy to make food from water and carbon dioxide in a process called photosynthesis.

mitochondrion

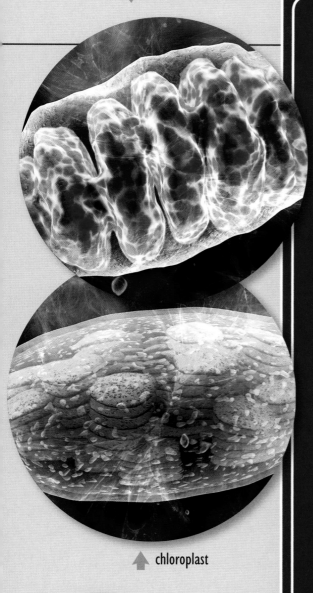
chloroplast

Rudolf Virchow (1821—1902)

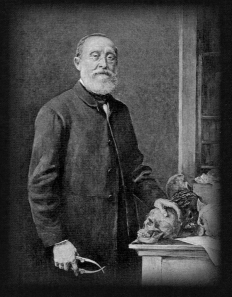

Rudolf Virchow was a German medical doctor. He was also considered the founder of cellular pathology, the study of how cells are involved in disease. He believed that disease was caused by cells, not organs or tissues. Virchow is best known for his contribution to the Cell Theory—that every cell originates from another cell.

Virchow is also known as the first person to identify leukemia. He also designed two hospitals and developed a standard method for performing autopsies.

Did You Know?

Rudolf Virchow studied the skulls of disabled persons to determine what caused their disabilities.

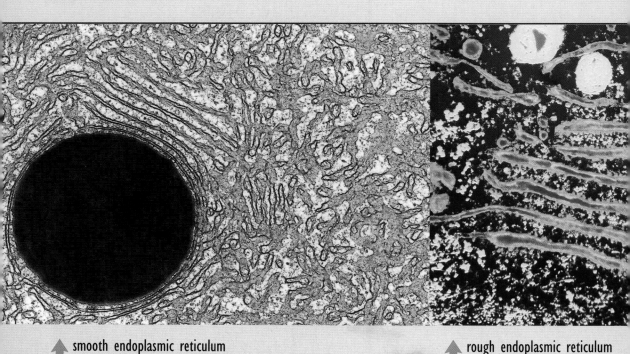

smooth endoplasmic reticulum

rough endoplasmic reticulum

Cell Factories

One of the cell's many jobs is to make new molecules. These molecules are produced in the endoplasmic reticulum (ER). The cell might keep the new molecules and use them, or it might send them out to be used by other cells. But before they exit the cell, the molecules must be "approved" by the Golgi apparatus. Getting molecules out of the cell is a complicated task.

There are two types of ER—smooth and rough. Smooth ER is a series of folded membranes. One of its jobs is to make substances called lipids, which store energy, build cell parts, and send messages. Rough ER makes lipids as well as proteins, the building blocks for many things a cell needs. Ribosomes are attached to the ouside of rough ER. They help assemble proteins

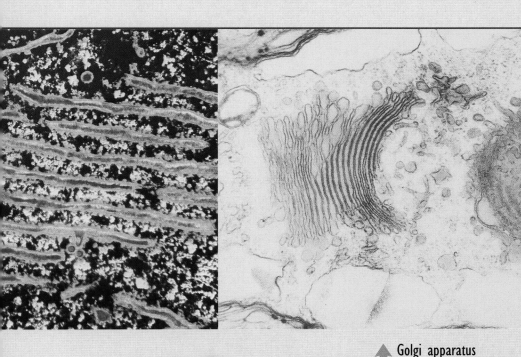

Golgi apparatus

by linking together chemical units called amino acids.

After the ER does its job, the lipids and proteins usually go to the Golgi apparatus, a stack of flattened membranes. The Golgi apparatus puts the lipids and proteins into vesicles, or small pouches, that prepare them for travel. They may now move to other parts of the cell, fuse with the cell membrane, or exit the cell.

Feeling Better?

Sometimes doctors prescribe antibiotics when a person is sick. Some kinds of antibiotics work by attacking a bacteria's ribosomes.

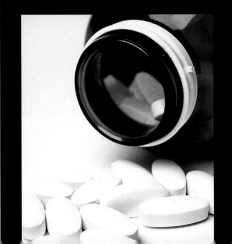

21

Cell Storage

Cells have storage places just like homes have cabinets and closets. These storage areas—called vacuoles—are bound by a single membrane. Vacuoles provide temporary storage for water, food, waste products, and other materials used by the cell.

Animal cells usually have many cell vacuoles. Plant cells usually have one very large vacuole that stores water for the plant. The vacuole in a plant cell increases in size when water is plentiful. It decreases when there is less water available for the plant.

The vacuole of a plant cell shrinks and expands. When it is full of water, the leaves are rigid. When a plant needs water, its leaves droop.

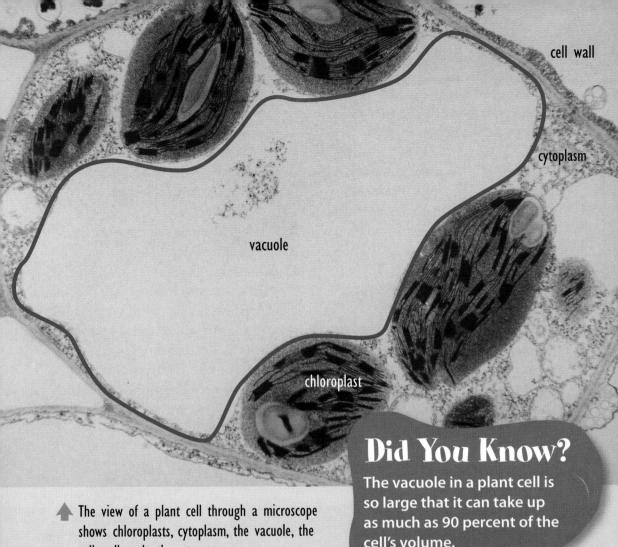

cell wall

cytoplasm

vacuole

chloroplast

The view of a plant cell through a microscope shows chloroplasts, cytoplasm, the vacuole, the cell wall, and other structures.

Cells also have organelles called lysosomes that recycle and remove unwanted materials. They contain chemicals that digest unwanted materials and break down old, worn-out cell parts, cell waste, and food molecules. It is very important that lysosomes have a membrane that separates the digestive chemicals from the rest of the cell. Otherwise the digestive chemicals would break down parts of the cell that are still needed.

23

Cell Movement

Although cells do not have legs and feet, some of them have appendages to help them move. Tiny hairlike projections called cilia help some cells move with their back-and-forth, wavelike motion.

Some cells do not move but still have cilia that help move fluid across a cell. For example, cilia help remove mucus from our lungs.

Another type of appendage is a flagellum. Flagella are the same thickness as cilia, but they are longer with a whiplike structure. Usually cells have only one flagellum. Cells with flagella move in a snakelike motion, allowing them to swim through liquid.

▼ cell with cilia

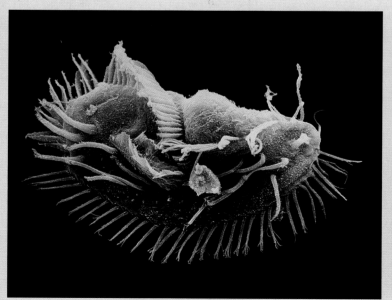

▼ cells with flagella

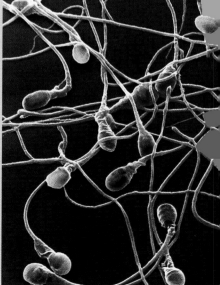

Rita Levi-Montalcini (1909—   )

Rita Levi-Montalcini was born in Italy to a traditional Jewish family. Her mother was a gifted painter. Her father was an electrical engineer and brilliant mathematician. Her father believed that a career would interfere with his daughter's role as a wife and mother. He would not allow any of his daughters to attend university. But Rita had a strong desire to go to medical school, and she begged her father to change his mind. Finally he allowed her to go. She attended medical school in Turin, Italy, from 1930 to 1936, graduating at the top of her class.

During World War II, Italian Jews were not allowed to practice medicine. So Rita conducted experiments secretly at home, researching nerve fibers in chicken embryos. After the war, she moved to the United States, where she was a professor at Washington University in St. Louis, Missouri, for 30 years. There she conducted further research on nerve cells and cancerous tissue. Her work has helped treat many types of injuries and diseases.

Levi-Montalcini has received many awards during her lifetime. In 1986, she and her research partner, Stanley Cohen, shared the Nobel Prize in medicine.

Cytoskeleton

Can you imagine your body without bones? You wouldn't be able to sit up, stand, or walk. Your skeleton provides support. Cells also have a kind of skeleton called a cytoskeleton, but it is not made of bones. Cells do not have a rigid or constant structure. But small hairlike fibers give shape to the cell and help it move.

There are three kinds of fibers that make up the cytoskeleton. The first is a hollow tube called a microtubule. The second is a microfilament, a

Microtubules are one type of fiber that makes up a cell's cytoskeleton.

solid rod made up of two twisted protein chains. The third type is a filament made of several chains of proteins coiled into a thick cable. These filaments are larger in diameter than microfilaments. Whatever the shape or makeup of the fibers, their job is to support the cell. Sometimes a cytoskeleton rebuilds itself, and the cell takes on a new shape.

Did You Know?

Some cells move when the fibers of the cytoskeleton break down and rebuild. This is often called cell crawling.

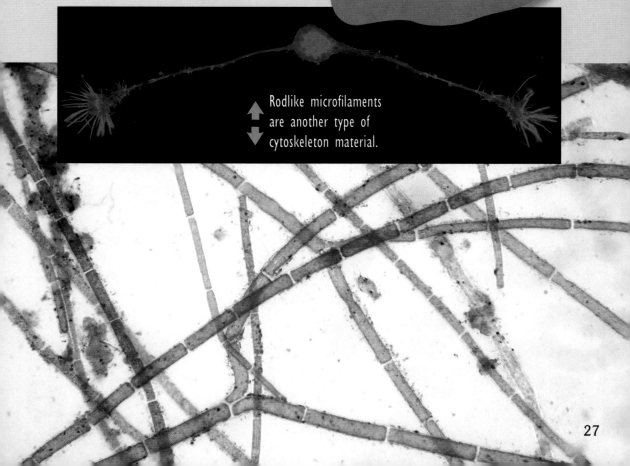

Rodlike microfilaments are another type of cytoskeleton material.

Making More Cells

Do you remember the three parts of the Cell Theory? All living things are made up of one or more cells; cells are the basic unit of life; and all cells come from other cells. New cells are made when a cell divides in a process called mitosis. However, something happens before mitosis: The cell makes a copy of its DNA. During mitosis, the cell splits into two daughter cells. Each daughter cell gets one copy of the DNA, producing two cells with DNA that is identical to the DNA in the original parent cell.

Cells produce new cells for many reasons. Since most animals and plants grow over time, the number of cells must increase. New cells also replace old or damaged cells. Some animal cells have to reproduce very quickly. For example, the cells in your stomach may only last a few days before stomach acid destroys them. Cells divide and make more cells rapidly before they are destroyed.

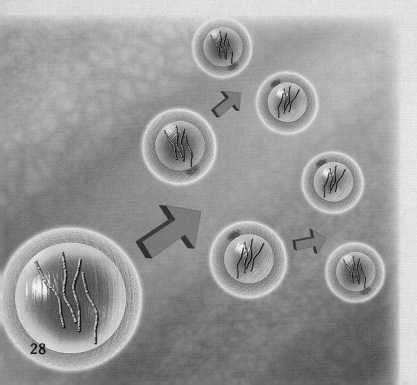

When a cell divides by mitosis, the result is two cells with identical DNA.

Elaine Fuchs
(1950—   )

Elaine Fuchs grew up in Illinois in a family of scientists who encouraged her to get a good education. Her father was a scientist, as well as her aunt and sister. Fuchs became a biochemist and then a university professor. She researches skin stem cells and studies genetic diseases such as skin cancer.

Fuchs was the first to use a research approach called reverse genetics. This process starts with knowing how a protein works and then looking at proteins that are defective, or don't work properly. Reverse genetics helps researchers identify diseases that occur with defective proteins.

Fuchs helped make dermatology—the study of skin and skin diseases—a modern-day science. She believes that it is important for children to be educated in science. She hopes children will be enthused about science like she is.

Did You Know?

Some bamboo plants can grow as much as a foot (30 centimeters) in a single day. New cells are made very quickly to cause such rapid growth.

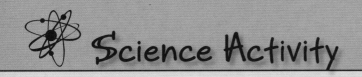
Make Your Own Light Microscope

Make this simple light microscope to see how early biologists examined their specimens.

Materials

- two magnifying glasses
- newspaper article
- photograph
- paper and pen to record your results

Procedure

1   Hold one magnifying glass just above the surface of the newspaper article. Then hold it above the photo. The print and image should appear larger.

2   Move the magnifying glass higher. See how the print and photo change. They should become blurred as you move the magnifying glass higher.

3   Return the magnifying glass to the original position. Place it just above the newspaper article.

4 Get the second magnifying glass. Place it between the first magnifying glass and your eyes.

5 Move the second magnifying glass up and down. Get the print in clear focus. How does it look?

6 Describe what happens. Does the print appear larger or smaller than it does when you used a single magnifying glass?

7 Record your results.

8 Repeat, using the photograph.

1665	Robert Hooke views the cell structure of cork under a microscope
1683	Anton van Leeuwenhoek discovers bacteria cells by studying tooth plaque
1831	Robert Brown reports his discovery of the nucleus, the command center of the cell
1838	Matthias Schleiden finds that plants are made up of cells
1839	Theodor Schwann discovers protective cells on nerve extensions; he calls them Schwann cells
1855	Rudolf Virchow states that all living cells come from other living cells
1953	Hans Adolf Krebs receives the Nobel Prize for his research on how energy is produced in cells (the Krebs Cycle)
1957	Joan Wright Goodman begins her pioneering stem cell research
1986	Rita Levi-Montalcini and Stanley Cohen share the Nobel Prize in medicine for their research on nerve cells
1995	Christiane Nüsslein-Volhard receives the Nobel Prize in medicine for her gene research in embryo development
2006	Elaine Fuchs receives the Dickson Prize in medicine for her pioneering research on reverse genetics

Glossary

amino acids—building blocks of protein

appendages—something added or attached to an entity of greater importance or size; for example, cells have cilia to help them move

biochemist—scientist who specializes in the study of chemical substances and vital processes occurring in living organisms

botanist—biologist specializing in the study of plants

cell—smallest unit of living things

Cell Theory—states that all living things are made up of one or more cells; cells are the basic unit of life; and all cells come from other cells

cellular pathology—study of disease origins in terms of cellular alterations

cellular respiration—process used by cells to break down food molecules into small units of energy

chlorophyll—chemical that plants use to capture the energy in sunlight

chloroplast—chlorophyll-containing organelle

chromosome—threadlike structure in the nucleus that carries the genes

cilia—small, hairlike extensions on some cells that are used for movement

concentration—strength of a solution

cytoplasm—fluid part of the cell where all cell functions are carried out

cytoskeleton—network of fibers that helps cells move, divide, and maintain their shape

diffusion—mixing together of different substances caused by the random motion of molecules and atoms

digest—to break down food into simpler chemical parts

DNA—deoxyribonucleic acid; molecule of which genes are made

embryo—animal that is developing either in its mother's womb or in an egg

endoplasmic reticulum—membrane-bound organelle that makes and moves materials around in a cell

flagellum—long, whiplike extension on some cells that is used for movement

function—natural purpose (or job) of something

gatekeeper—someone or something that controls what can come in and what can go out

Golgi apparatus—membrane-bound organelle that modifies materials

lipid—substance such as fat that dissolves in alcohol but not in water and is an important part of living cells

lysosome—membrane-bound organelle that contains chemicals for digesting unwanted cell materials

membrane—thin, flexible layer of tissue covering surfaces of animal or plant cells

mitochondria—membrane-bound organelle where cellular respiration occurs

mitosis—process of cell division

nucleus—command center of the cell that gives instructions to the other parts of the cell

organelle—specialized part of a cell that has one or more specific functions

photosynthesis—process by which plants make food using sunlight, carbon dioxide, and water

pigment—substance that gives something a particular color when it is present in it or is added to it

proteins—fundamental components of all living cells that are essential in the diet of animals for the growth and repair of tissues

reproduction—production of young plants and animals through a sexual or asexual process

reverse genetics—process of identifying and isolating genes responsible for a particular disease

Schwann cells—cells that make up the protective covering of nerve cell extensions

substance—that which has mass and occupies space

vacuole—large space in a plant cell that stores water and food

Robert Brown (1773–1885)
Scottish botanist who identified more than 2,000
new plant species; identified and named the nucleus,
the round-shaped command center in the middle of a
plant cell

Stanley Cohen (1922–   )
American scientist who discovered growth factors,
chemicals in the body that stimulate cell growth;
co-winner, with Rita Levi-Montalcini, of the Nobel Prize
in medicine in 1986

Elaine Fuchs (1950–   )
American biochemist who has studied genetic diseases
and cancers of the skin; helped make dermatology a
modern-day science

Joan Wright Goodman (1925–2006)
American scientist who is known for her pioneering
research on stem cells; paved the way for modern stem
cell research when she identified stem cells in the blood
of mice

Robert Hooke (1635–1703)
English scientist credited with observing the first
cells under a microscope and naming them cellulae
(cells); drew detailed images of his observations using
a microscope and published them in 1665 in his book
Micrographia

Hans Adolf Krebs (1900–1981)
German medical doctor and biochemist who studied
how cells turn glucose into energy; won the 1953 Nobel
Prize in medicine for his discovery of the Krebs Cycle

Anton van Leeuwenhoek (1632–1723)
Dutch scientist who made hundreds of microscopes and observed bacteria cells for the first time; he is commonly known as the father of microbiology

Rita Levi-Montalcini (1909–   )
Italian medical doctor who researched chicken embryos in secret during World War II; conducted research on nerve cells and cancerous tissue, helping in the treatment of many types of injuries and diseases; co-winner, with Stanley Cohen, of the Nobel Prize in medicine in 1986

Christiane Nüsslein-Volhard (1942–   )
German scientist who studied fruit flies to learn more about the genes that cause birth defects; received the Nobel Prize in medicine in 1995

Matthias Schleiden (1804–1881)
German lawyer and amateur botanist whose discovery that plants are made of cells became the first part of the Cell Theory

Theodor Schwann (1810–1882)
German physiologist who discovered the cells that cover and protect nerve cell extensions; named the cells Schwann cells; contributed to the Cell Theory

Rudolf Virchow (1821–1902)
German medical doctor considered to be the founder of cellular pathology; his discovery that cells come from other cells became the third part of the Cell Theory

DuPrau, Jeanne. *Cells.* San Diego: Kidhaven Press, 2002.

Kalman, Bobbie. *Photosynthesis: Changing Sunlight Into Food.* New York: Crabtree Publishing, 2005.

Snedden, Robert. *Animals: Multicelled Life.* Oxford: Heinemann Library, 2002.

Snedden, Robert. *Plants & Fungi: Multicelled Life.* Oxford: Heinemann Library, 2002.

Stille, Darlene R. *Animal Cells: The Smallest Units of Life.* Minneapolis: Compass Point Books, 2006.

Stille, Darlene R. *Plant Cells: The Building Blocks of Plants.* Minneapolis: Compass Point Books, 2006.

On the Web

For more information on this topic, use FactHound.

1. Go to *www.facthound.com*

2. Type in this book ID: 0756539544

3. Click on the *Fetch It* button.

FactHound will find the best Web sites for you.

Index

About the Author

Kimberly Fekany Lee

Kimberly Fekany Lee earned her B.S. in chemistry from the University of Florida. She then studied axis formation in zebrafish to earn her Ph.D. in molecular biology from Vanderbilt University. Lee worked as a high school science teacher in Ft. Lauderdale, Florida, before moving to the Chicago area. She is currently a freelance science writer and editor, residing in La Grange, Illinois. She is married and enjoys sharing her love of science with her three children.

Image Credits